Customer Service
Exam Prep Guide

PEARSON
Prentice Hall

Upper Saddle River, New Jersey
Columbus, Ohio

NATIONAL
RESTAURANT
ASSOCIATION
SOLUTIONS ™

DISCLAIMER:

The information presented in this publication is provided for informational purposes only and is not intended to provide legal advice or establish standards of reasonable behavior. Customers who develop food safety-related or operational policies and procedures are urged to obtain the advice and guidance of legal counsel. Although **National Restaurant Association Solutions, LLC (NRA Solutions)** endeavors to include accurate and current information compiled from sources believed to be reliable, **NRA Solutions**, and its **licensor**, **the National Restaurant Association Educational Foundation (NRAEF)**, distributors, and agents make no representations or warranties as to the accuracy, currency, or completeness of the information. No responsibility is assumed or implied by the NRAEF, NRA Solutions, distributors, or agents for any damage or loss resulting from inaccuracies or omissions or any actions taken or not taken based on the content of this publication.

Sample questions are designed to familiarize the student with format, length and style of the examination questions, and represent only a sampling of topic coverage. The performance level on sample questions does not guarantee passing of a ManageFirst Program examination. Further, the distribution of sample exam questions with their focus on particular areas of subject matter within a ManageFirst Competency Guide is not necessarily reflective of how the questions will be distributed across subject matter on the actual correlating ManageFirst exam.

Visit www.restaurant.org for information on other National Restaurant Association Solutions products and programs.

ManageFirst Program™, ServSafe®, and ServSafe Alcohol® are registered trademarks or trademarks of the National Restaurant Association Educational Foundation, used under license by National Restaurant Association Solutions, LLC a wholly owned subsidiary of the National Restaurant Association.

ISBN-13: 978-0-13-812689-6
ISBN-10:   0-13-812689-5

10 9 8 7 6 5

Contents

How to Take the ManageFirst Examination

The ability to take tests effectively is a learned skill. There are specific things you can do to prepare yourself physically and mentally for an exam. This section helps you prepare and do your best on the ManageFirst Examination.

I. BEFORE THE EXAM

A. How to Study

Study the right material the right way. There is a lot of information and material in each course. How do you know what to study so you are prepared for the exam? This guide highlights what you need to know.

1. **Read the Introduction to each *Competency Guide*.** The beginning section of each guide explains the features and how it is organized.

2. **Look at how each chapter is organized and take clues from the book.**

   - *The text itself is important.* If the text is bold, large, or italicized you can be sure it is a key point that you should understand.

   - *The very first page tells you what you will learn.*

     Inside This Chapter: This tells you at a high level what will be covered in the chapter. Make sure you understand what each section covers. If you have studied the chapter but cannot explain what each section pertains to, you need to review that material.

Learning Objectives: After completing each chapter, you should be able to accomplish the specific goals and demonstrate what you have learned after reading the material. The practice exam as well as the actual exam questions relate to these learning objectives.

■ *Quizzes and Tests*

Test Your Knowledge: This is a pretest found at the beginning of each chapter to see how much you already know. Take this quiz to help you determine which areas you need to study and focus on.

■ *Key Terms* are listed at the beginning of each chapter and set in bold the first time they are referred to in the chapter. These terms—new and specific to the topic or ones you are already familiar with—are key to understanding the chapter's content. When reviewing the material, look for the key terms you don't know or understand and review the corresponding paragraph.

■ *Exhibits* visually depict key concepts and include charts, tables, photographs, and illustrations. As you review each chapter, find out how well you can explain the concepts illustrated in the exhibits.

■ *Additional Exercises*

Think About It sidebars are designed to provoke further thought and/or discussion and require understanding of the topics.

Activity boxes are designed to check your understanding of the material and help you apply your knowledge. The activities relate to a learning objective.

■ *Summary* reviews all the important concepts in the chapter and helps you retain and master the material.

3. **Attend Review Sessions or Study Groups**. Review sessions, if offered, cover material that will most likely be on the test. If separate review sessions are not offered, make sure you attend class the day before the exam. Usually, the instructor will review the material during this class. If you are a social learner, study with other students; discussing the topics with other students may help your comprehension and retention.

4. **Review the Practice Questions,** which are designed to help you prepare for the exam. Sample questions are designed to familiarize the student with the format, length, and style of the exam questions, and represent only a sampling of topic coverage on the final exam. The performance level on sample questions does not guarantee passing of a ManageFirst Program exam.

B. *How to Prepare Physically and Mentally*

Make sure you are ready to perform your best during the exam. Many students do everything wrong when preparing for an exam. They stay up all night, drink coffee to stay awake, or take sleep aids which leave them groggy and tired on test day.

There are practical things to do to be at your best. If you were an athlete preparing for a major event, what would you do to prepare yourself? You wouldn't want to compete after staying up all night or drinking lots of caffeine. The same holds true when competing with your brain!

1. **Get plenty of sleep.** Lack of sleep makes it difficult to focus and recall information. Some tips to help you get a good night's sleep are:

   - Make sure you have studied adequately enough days before the exam so that you do not need to cram and stay up late the night before the test.
   - Eat a good dinner the night before and a good breakfast the day of the exam.
   - Do not drink alcohol or highly-caffeinated drinks.
   - Exercise during the day, but not within four hours of bedtime.
   - Avoid taking sleep aids.

2. **Identify and control anxiety.** It is important to know the difference between actual test anxiety and anxiety caused by not being prepared.

Test anxiety is an actual physical reaction. If you know the information when you are **not** under pressure but feel physically sick and cannot recall information during the exam, you probably suffer from test anxiety. In this case, you may need to learn relaxation techniques or get some counseling. The key is how you react under pressure.

If you cannot recall information during reviews or the practice exam when you are not under pressure, you have not committed the information to memory and need to study more.

- Make sure you are as prepared as possible. (See "Anxiety Caused by Lack of Preparation")
- Take the exam with a positive attitude.
- Do not talk to other students who may be pessimistic or negative about the exam.
- Know what helps you relax and do it (chewing gum, doodling, breathing exercises).
- Make sure you understand the directions. Ask the instructor questions *before* the test begins.
- The instructor or proctor may only talk to you if you have defective materials or need to go to the restroom. They cannot discuss any questions.
- The instructor or proctor may continuously monitor the students so do not be nervous if they walk around the room.
- Know the skills described in Section II, During the Test.

3. **Anxiety Caused by Lack of Preparation.** The best way to control anxiety due to lack of preparation is focus on the exam. Whenever possible, you should know and do the following:

- Know the location of the exam and how to get there.
- Know if it is a paper-and-pencil test or an online exam. Pencils may be available but bring sufficient number 2 pencils if taking the paper-and-pencil version of the exam.
- If it is an online exam you may need your email address, if you have one, to receive results.
- You are prohibited from using purses, books, papers, pagers, cell phones, or other recording devices during the exam.
- Calculators and scratch paper may be used, if needed. Be sure your calculator is working properly and has fresh batteries.
- The exam is not a timed; however, it is usually completed in less than two hours.
- Take the sample exam so you know what format, style, and content to expect.
- Arrive early so you don't use valuable testing time to unpack.

II. DURING THE TEST

An intent of National Restaurant Association Solutions' ManageFirst exams is to make sure you have met certain learning objectives. If you are physically prepared, have studied the material, and taken the practice exam, you should find the ManageFirst exams to be very valid and fair. Remember, successful test taking is a skill. Understanding the different aspects of test preparation and exam taking will help ensure your best performance.

A. Test Taking Strategies

- Preview the exam for a quick overview of the length and questions.
- Do not leave any question unanswered.
- Answer the questions you are sure of first.

- Stop and check occasionally to make sure you are putting your answer in the correct place on the answer sheet. If you are taking an online exam, you will view one question at a time.
- Do not spend too much time on any one question. If you do not know the answer after reasonable consideration, move on and come back to it later.
- Make note of answers about which you are unsure so you can return to them.
- Review the exam at the end to check your answers and make sure all questions are answered.

B. Strategies for Answering Multiple-Choice Questions

Multiple-choice tests are objective. The correct answer is there, you just need to identify it.

- Try to answer the question before you look at the options.
- Use the process of elimination. Eliminate the answers you know are incorrect.
- Your first response is usually correct.

III. AFTER THE EXAM

Learn from each exam experience so you can do better on the next. If you did not perform on the exam as you expected, determine the reason. Was it due to lack of studying or preparation? Were you unable to control your test anxiety? Were you not focused enough because you were too tired? Identifying the reason allows you to spend more time on that aspect before your next exam. Use the information to improve on your next exam.

If you do not know the reason, you should schedule a meeting with the instructor. As all NRA Solutions ManageFirst exams are consistent, it is important to understand and improve your exam performance. If you cannot identify your problem areas, your errors will most likely be repeated on consecutive exams.

IV. EXAM DAY DETAILS

The information contained in this section will help ensure that you are able to take the exam on the scheduled test day and that you know what to expect and are comfortable about taking the exam.

- Have your photo identification available.
- Anyone with special needs must turn in an *Accommodation Request* to the instructor at least 10 days prior to the exam to receive approval and allow time for preparations. *If needs are not known 10 days prior, you may not be able to take the exam on the scheduled test day.*
- A bilingual English-native language dictionary may be used by anyone who speaks English as a second language. The dictionary will be inspected to make sure there are no notes or extra papers in it.
- If you are ill and must leave the room after the exam has begun you must turn in your materials to the instructor or proctor. If you are able to return, your materials will be returned to you and you may complete the exam. If it is an online exam you must close your browser and if the exam has not been graded yet, login in again when you return.
- Restroom breaks are allowed. Only one person may go at a time and all materials must be turned in prior to leaving the room and picked up when you return; or you must close your browser and login again for online exams.
- Make-up tests may be available if you are unable to take the exam on test day. Check with your instructor for details.
- If you are caught cheating you will not receive a score and must leave the exam location.

Customer Service
Chapter Summaries and Objectives

Chapter 1 The Importance of Customer Service to Your Business

Summary

Customer service impacts all aspects of business, such as revenue, profit, cost, the guest, and the employee. High-quality customer service consists of service and hospitality, which includes the products provided and the feeling customers take with them. Influencing the customer's perception of value and consistently meeting or exceeding customer expectations leads to customer loyalty and profit. The best way to accomplish this is to implement and manage a high-quality customer service system that ensures your marketing promises are fulfilled. The restaurant and foodservice industry is extremely competitive. High-quality customer service can be the competitive edge that allows a business to set the standard and become the benchmark for the competition. Creating positive impressions, moments of truth, and an overall positive cycle of service will help you achieve the many benefits of high-quality customer service. Customer service can impact many areas of the operation such as loyalty, marketing, reputation, turnover, costs, and profits.

After completing this chapter, you should be able to:
- Explain the importance of customer service to a restaurant or foodservice operation.
- Differentiate between hospitality and service.
- List and explain the impact of customer service.
- Identify the relationship between customer satisfaction and customer loyalty.
- Define moments of truth.
- Identify the cycle of service.

Chapter 2 Basic Concepts for High-Quality Customer Service

Summary

In today's competitive market, the successful owner or manager in the restaurant and foodservice industry needs to attract and retain customers, both internal (employees) and external (guests). Customers are involved in an input-output relationship with each other all the time. Satisfying internal customers greatly improves the chances of satisfying external customers. Developing, implementing, and managing a system that enables you to provide high-quality customer service by understanding how different aspects of the operation affect each other is one of the keys to a successful career in the restaurant and foodservice industry. Understanding the service-profit chain and taking a systems management approach to high-quality customer service is the most effective and efficient way to satisfy internal and external customers and be profitable over time.

After completing this chapter, you should be able to:
- Explain the high-quality customer service system.
- Define and distinguish between internal and external customers.
- Describe the systems management approach.
- Describe the service-profit chain.
- Explain how the service-profit chain relates to the high-quality customer service system.

Chapter 3 Identifying Customer Expectations

Summary

Customer expectations can change often. A properly designed, implemented, and managed high-quality customer service system should have processes in place to continuously monitor and record internal and external customer expectations. The tools and methods for collecting, recording, and analyzing customer service data should also be adjusted over time. The best source of information is the customer. If methods and tools are used properly, both internal and external customers will be very accommodating in providing the valuable feedback necessary to stay current with customer demands and expectations.

After completing this chapter, you should be able to:
■ Identify ways to staff properly to ensure prompt, friendly, and courteous customer service.
■ Explain the importance of determining customers' expectations.
■ Describe internal and external customer expectations.
■ List the tools and methods for identifying customer expectations and feedback.
■ Explain the importance of gathering feedback from customers.
■ List the types of feedback to be obtained from internal and external customers.

Chapter 4 Ensuring Consistent Service Value

Summary

Delivering consistent customer service and creating value help lead to the customer satisfaction and customer loyalty components in the service-profit chain. Communication, suggestive selling, flow of service, and service recovery are tasks that support consistent customer service and creation of value.

Communication is a complex activity and there are many factors involved with effective communication. Many service issues are the result of miscommunication, which can be caused by misunderstanding and other factors. Communication is a two-way process of sending and receiving information, and listening is an important aspect of communication. Staff training to ensure effective communication is management's responsibility. Regular training at staff meetings and preshift meetings can be effective methods to reinforce communication techniques.

Guests want to maximize their dining experience. The staff should help achieve this. Suggestive selling is one tool servers have to enhance a guest's dining experience and meet or exceed expectations. Pace and flow of service is a factor that influences a customer's perception of value. Your operation should have a system of standards and procedures for ensuring that products are served promptly, as ordered, and to standards. The more effectively customers are served, the more they feel their time is respected and appreciated.

Correctly and courteously handling customer complaints and service recovery are critical aspects of customer service. Customers are likely to be more loyal if their complaints are resolved in a satisfactory way. This reinforces the fact that it is in the best interests of both customers and management to resolve complaints positively.

After completing this chapter, you should be able to:
- Ensure proper and effective communication with the customer.
- Maximize guest satisfaction through suggestive selling.
- Ensure that products are served promptly, as ordered, and to standards.
- Manage the pace and flow of service.
- Ensure satisfactory resolution of customer complaints.

Chapter 5 Ensuring Profit

Summary

Having a system for accepting a variety of payment forms is important to the success of any restaurant or foodservice operation. The payment system should be secure for both the business and the guest. Technology can solve many problems; however, improperly using technology can create new problems. Installing the appropriate system for collecting and recording payments and then properly training the appropriate staff on the system will contribute to satisfied internal and external customers.

Convenience is a growing trend in foodservice. Therefore, to-go, delivery, and drive-through orders are important parts of the sales mix. Proper procedures and training in this area are important to maintaining a competitive edge.

After completing this chapter, you should be able to:
- Demonstrate the proper use of payment procedures.
- Describe security issues dealing with credit or debit card payment.
- Explain point-of-sale issues affecting profit.
- Explain operational and cost-control issues for to-go, delivery, and drive-through orders.

Customer Service
Practice Questions

Please note the numbers in parentheses following each question. They represent the chapter and page number, respectively, where the content in found in the ManageFirst Competency Guide.

IMPORTANT: These sample questions are designed to familiarize the student with format, length and style of the examination questions, and represent only a sampling of topic coverage.

The grid below represents how the *actual* exam questions will be divided across content areas on the corresponding ManageFirst Program exam.

Customer Service	1.	The Importance of Customer Service to Your Business	7
	2.	Basic Concepts for High-Quality Customer Service	6
	3.	Identifying Customer Expectations	9
	4.	Ensuring Consistent Service Value	14
	5.	Ensuring Profit	14
		Total No. of Questions	**50**

The performance level on sample questions does not guarantee passing of a ManageFirst Program examination. Further, the distribution of sample exam questions with their focus on particular areas of subject matter within a ManageFirst Competency Guide is not necessarily reflective of how the questions will be distributed across subject matter on the actual correlating ManageFirst exam.

1. A restaurant keeps losing its employees because they are frustrated with the poor training. They aren't sure what to do themselves, and there are many errors due to others not receiving adequate training. Employees have regularly asked for some explanation of tasks and responsibilities, but the manager has been too busy to provide any job aids or policies. What is this problem due to? (3, 42)
   A. Poor tools and equipment
   B. The manager hiring the wrong people
   C. The manager not addressing internal customer expectations
   D. The manager being too concerned with doing things "by the book"

2. A restaurant manager holds regular staff meetings. Occasionally employees are asked to role-play how they would handle actual situations where customers had complaints. Why is role-playing beneficial to the employees? (4, 76)
   A. It is a good way for employees to get to know each other.
   B. They can practice acting genuinely so the customers think they are concerned.
   C. Most complaints are repetitive so the role-playing shouldn't be necessary.
   D. They can practice their listening skills, patience, and staying calm with an angry customer.

3. Since fewer people are paying with personal checks, why is it important to still include this type of payment training? (5, 87)
   A. Suggestive selling usually requires payment by personal check.
   B. Restaurants are trying to encourage more payment with personal checks.
   C. It is the safest form of payment since you must have the money in the bank in order to write a check.
   D. Employees are not familiar with them and may not know if they are completed correctly.

4. Revenue and growth are linked in a high-quality customer service system. When a business successfully satisfies internal and external customers, costs are reduced and productivity is increased. This relationship is called (2, 30)
   A. service recovery.
   B. employee motivation.
   C. the service-profit chain.
   D. the four parts of high-quality customer service.

5. A person's past experiences can affect how they send or receive information. It is one of many factors in their (4, 59)
   A. field of experience.
   B. range of expectations.
   C. physical ability.
   D. new employee training.

6. A customer asks a greeter whether it is possible to get a surprise birthday cake served at the end of the meal. The greeter says he will let the server know. The greeter tells the server but at the end of the meal the birthday cake does not come. What role in the communication process was ineffective? (4, 59)
   A. The customer was not an effective sender.
   B. The customer was not an effective receiver.
   C. The greeter was not an effective sender.
   D. The greeter was not an effective receiver.

7. One greeter leads the guests to a table and tells them a server will be with them soon. A different greeter leads guests to a table and notices that their child has a special ribbon pinned on his shirt. The greeter asks what it is for and congratulates the child on the award. The difference between these experiences is how the greeter performed. What is this also called? (1, 5)
   A. Service
   B. Efficiency
   C. Hospitality
   D. Effectiveness

8. A group of young professionals visit your restaurant often because there is a quiet section where they can plug in their computers and get some work done. The restaurant created this area specifically for this purpose because they are near a business section of town. What is this is an example of? (3, 44)
   A. Competitive analysis
   B. Knowing and satisfying customer expectations
   C. Taking advantage of meal specials to attract certain demographics
   D. Engaging in conversation with customers to understand their needs

9. All restaurants have a service system with aspects such as reservations, table setup, food delivery, check presentation, and other tasks that affect the pace and flow. The pace and flow can differ greatly between restaurants but what is it always about? (4, 68)
   A. Timing
   B. Food quality
   C. Customer expectations
   D. Getting customers in and out as quickly as possible

10. Which of the following actions would create a cash overage to occur? (5, 87)
    A. A guest was not given enough change.
    B. A quick-change artist confused the cashier.
    C. An employee stole money from the register.
    D. A bill was placed under the drawer and not counted.

11. The accumulation of all the opportunities to form an opinion from the beginning to the end of a dining experience is called (1, 15)
    A. first impression.
    B. cycle of service.
    C. high-quality customer service.
    D. competitive point of difference.

12. A greeter notices that a person sitting near a window is holding up her hand to block the sun that is shining directly on them. The greeter asks the customer if she would like the shade lowered. The customer agrees and is very appreciative since she didn't notice there was a shade. How did the greeter receive information about this customer's problem? (3, 44)
    A. By engaging in conversation
    B. Observing the guest's behavior
    C. Reading comment cards of other guests
    D. Questioning guests about their experience

13. What is one type of behavior that can help improve communication? (4, 63)
    A. Being assertive
    B. Having credibility
    C. Interrupting to check for understanding
    D. Using jargon and slang to make a point

14. What is service recovery? (4, 74)
    A. A method to make sure there are enough servers if some call in sick
    B. Standards and guidelines for handling recovery of damaged property
    C. An operation's response to a dissatisfied customer to make them satisfied again
    D. A process to make sure a business is reimbursed if service is required on equipment

15. A restaurant that hires a lot of young employees offers a scholarship program and more vacation than its competitors. This is an example of which of the four rights? (3, 38)
    A. Hire right
    B. Train right
    C. Compensate right
    D. Retain right

16. Why is suggestive selling advantageous to the server specifically? (4, 66)
    A. It can increase customer satisfaction so tips may be increased.
    B. It gives them something to talk about with their guests.
    C. Guest satisfaction is increased and therefore so is productivity.
    D. It helps prepare the server for a management position.

17. What is an acceptable way to handle a customer complaint? (4, 75)
    A. Take ownership for resolving the complaint
    B. Ask them to go to the Web site and fill out a complaint form
    C. Passively listen to the guest to make sure it doesn't interfere with regular tasks
    D. Apologize to the guest but defend the actions if the customer is "not right"

18. Influencing the customer's perception of value and consistently meeting or exceeding customer expectations leads to (1, 19)
    A. a bad reputation.
    B. a cycle of service.
    C. employee turnover.
    D. customer loyalty.

19. A restaurant has a training program for all new employees where they spend time with the greeter, the server, the kitchen staff, and the bussers to see what everyone does. This helps the new employee see how the processes interact and how his tasks impact everyone else. What is this an example of? (2, 29)
    A. Multi-tasking by trainees
    B. Cross-functional knowledge
    C. High-quality customer service
    D. Systems-management approach

20. High-quality customer service will cause what to decrease? (1, 9)
    A. Cost
    B. Profits
    C. Loyalty
    D. Reputation

21. What is the process called of matching recorded sales against actual payments received? (5, 91)
    A. Reconciliation
    B. Service-profit chain
    C. Service recovery
    D. Fraud control

22. What term best describes anyone inside an organization who receives product, services, or information from someone else to complete his or her work? (2, 25)
    A. Trainee
    B. Manager
    C. Internal customer
    D. External customer

23. According to the Competency Guide, what does customer loyalty mean? (1, 10)
    A. Customer will only dine at your restaurant.
    B. Customers prefer your restaurant to all similar restaurants.
    C. Customer will not ever say anything bad about your restaurant.
    D. Customers will continue to dine at your restaurant even if the service is continuously bad.

24. Suggestive selling is beneficial to the company because it can increase profits. Why is it beneficial to the customer? (4, 66)
    A. They won't need to read the menu.
    B. The customer will be less inclined to order dessert.
    C. The customer may not be aware of certain options.
    D. The customer gets an opportunity to talk to the server.

25. Which of the following represents a food cost ratio of 33%? Round to the nearest whole percentage. (5, 83)
    A. Food cost is $4 and dinner price is $8
    B. Food cost is $4 and dinner price is $12
    C. Food cost is $4 and dinner price is $16
    D. Food cost is $4 and dinner price is $20

26. When processing credit card payments, the staff should be trained to (5, 90)
   A. automatically add tip to the transaction.
   B. give the card to the manager for verification.
   C. verify that the signature on the receipt matches the signature on the card.
   D. return the card to the person you presented the check to regardless of the actual owner.

27. According to the Competency Guide, when analyzing comment cards, what is important to realize about the people that are most likely to fill them out? (3, 49)
   A. They are internal customers.
   B. They are people who are regular customers.
   C. They are people who have had a negative experience.
   D. They are people who have had a positive experience.

28. According to the Competency Guide, who should handle a complaint to ensure a successful service recovery plan? (4, 75)
   A. The manager should be the only person allowed to handle a complaint regardless of company policy.
   B. Only the employee who has spent the most time with the customer should address the issue.
   C. Anyone can handle it, as long as no one gets blamed for the problem.
   D. Each operation should have its own policy and everyone should be trained and understand who will take responsibility.

29. What is it called when a cash register entry has to be corrected or cancelled? (5, 85)
   A. Exchange
   B. Return
   C. Void
   D. Reconciliation

30. Workplace design, job design, employee development, and recognition are all examples of supportive processes for what? (2, 31)
   A. The service profit chain
   B. Input-output relationships
   C. Return-on-investment programs
   D. OSHA requirements for employee satisfaction

Customer Service
Answer Key to Practice Questions

1.	C	16.	A
2.	D	17.	A
3.	D	18.	D
4.	C	19.	B
5.	A	20.	A
6.	C	21.	A
7.	C	22.	C
8.	B	23.	B
9.	A	24.	C
10.	A	25.	B
11.	B	26.	C
12.	B	27.	C
13.	B	28.	D
14.	C	29.	C
15.	C	30.	A

Customer Service
Explanations to the Answers for the Practice Questions

Question 1
Answer A is wrong. The employees have specifically said it is the training.
Answer B is wrong. If needs are not met many people will become frustrated.
Answer C is correct. Employees are internal customers and their needs must be understood and met.
Answer D is wrong. Employees cannot do things by the book if they have not been trained.

Question 2
Answer A is wrong. The purpose of role-playing is to experience and practice different skills.
Answer B is wrong. Customers can tell if you are not genuine.
Answer C is wrong. Complaints should be addressed so they do not occur again.
Answer D is correct. The more employees can practice interactions the better prepared they will be to handle different situations.

Question 3
Answer A is wrong. Purchases due to suggestive selling can be paid for with any form of payment.
Answer B is wrong. Restaurants do not prefer personal checks since they take time to clear.
Answer C is wrong. Checks can be written if there is no money in the bank to cover the amount.
Answer D is correct. Employees may not write checks and therefore need training to understand if they are completed correctly and to ask for the correct identification.

Question 4

Answer A is wrong. Service recovery pertains to customer complaints.

Answer B is wrong. Employee motivation only relates to the internal customers.

Answer C is correct. The service-profit chain is a model to explain the relationship between revenue and growth.

Answer D is wrong. The four parts of high-quality customer service are identifying customer expectations, consistently exceeding customer expectations, providing products and services that create value for the customer, and creating profit for the organization.

Question 5

Answer A is correct. Field of experience consists of all the things a person has gone through that affect either forming or interpreting a message. It is their perspective.

Answer B is wrong. What a person expects does not impact how a message is received.

Answer C is wrong. Physical ability usually does not impact communication.

Answer D is wrong. New employee training is information related to the job, it is not related to a person's past experiences.

Question 6

Answer A is wrong. The customer was an effective sender because the greeter got the message and forwarded it to the server.

Answer B is wrong. The customer was not a receiver in this interaction.

Answer C is correct. The greeter may have sent the message but because no action was taken it is not certain if the server received the message.

Answer D is wrong. The greeter was an effective receiver because he passed the message on to the server, although ineffectively.

Question 7

Answer A is wrong. Service is what the greeter provides.

Answer B is wrong. Efficiency is how well or quickly a task is performed.

Answer C is correct. Hospitality is how a service makes a customer feel.

Answer D is wrong. Effectiveness is how well the service met the customer's needs.

Question 8

Answer A is wrong. We do not know if the competition was analyzed.

Answer B is correct. The specific need was a meeting place and the restaurant created a work area to meet this need.

Answer C is wrong. Meal specials do not meet the need for a place to meet.

Answer D is wrong. There may have been conversation to determine the needs but the important point is that the restaurant created the area in response to their needs.

Question 9

Answer A is correct. Timing of all these factors must be managed regardless of whether it is a quick-service, full-service, or fine-dining experience.

Answer B is wrong. Food quality is not a factor in how smoothly things run.

Answer C is wrong. The pace and flow is based on the type of restaurant it is. The customer's expectations may not match the dining experience provided by this type of restaurant.

Answer D is wrong. Some restaurants provide a lengthy dining experience.

Question 10

Answer A is correct. If a guest was not given enough change there would be too much money in the register.

Answer B is wrong. A quick-change artist would cause a cash shortage.

Answer C is wrong. Theft would create a cash shortage.

Answer D is wrong. A cash shortage would occur if a bill was not counted.

Question 11

Answer A is wrong. The first impression is one of all the moments in the cycle of service.

Answer B is correct. The cycle of service is every moment from the beginning to the end of the dining experience.

Answer C is wrong. High-quality customer service is provided to the customer during the entire cycle of service.

Answer D is wrong. A competitive point of difference is the difference between restaurants.

Question 12

Answer A is wrong. Conversation was not needed to identify the problem.

Answer B is correct. The greeter saw the guest blocking the sun.

Answer C is wrong. This example does not indicate there were any cards.

Answer D is wrong. The problem was discovered without talking to the guests.

Question 13

Answer A is wrong. Assertiveness can intimidate some customers.

Answer B is correct. Credibility is critical when the communication involves solving a problem or providing information.

Answer C is wrong. The receiver should not interrupt; rather he or she should wait until the sender has completed the message, then check for understanding.

Answer D is wrong. Slang and jargon should be avoided since not everyone understands the meaning of these terms or phrases.

Question 14

Answer A is wrong. Service recovery refers to customer service, not employees.

Answer B is wrong. Service recovery does not refer to physical property; it refers to customer satisfaction.

Answer C is correct. Service Recovery is an operation's response to a complaint to return to a state of customer satisfaction.

Answer D is wrong. Service recovery refers to customer service, not repair service.

Question 15
Answer A is wrong. Hire right refers to the selection of the employees.

Answer B is wrong. Offering a scholarship program and more vacation is not related to training new employees.

Answer C is correct. Compensation includes benefits, incentive programs, flexible schedules, and rewards programs.

Answer D is wrong. Retain right refers to adequately providing things other than compensation.

Question 16
Answer A is correct. A customer's experience can be enhanced by suggestive selling because they may be unaware of some things or may need help on choices.

Answer B is wrong. The purpose is not to create conversation but to offer something in particular to the guest.

Answer C is wrong. Guest satisfaction does not necessarily affect productivity.

Answer D is wrong. Suggestive selling may help employee development but it does not provide management skills.

Question 17
Answer A is correct. Operations with excellent service recovery have empowered employees that take responsibility for resolving customer complaints.

Answer B is wrong. It is important to handle customer complaints immediately. The customer should not have to seek a solution. The restaurant should initiate it and make sure it is resolved.

Answer C is wrong. The guest shouldn't feel that they are not being listened to.

Answer D is wrong. To the customer they are always right. Action should be taken to satisfy the customer and not try to defend what caused the dissatisfaction.

Question 18

Answer A is wrong. Meeting or exceeding customer expectations will create a good reputation.

Answer B is wrong. Cycle of service is all the opportunities a customer has to form an opinion.

Answer C is wrong. Employee turnover occurs when the needs of internal customers are not met.

Answer D is correct. Customers will prefer your restaurant to others if they are consistently satisfied or impressed.

Question 19

Answer A is wrong. Multi-tasking means performing multiple tasks at the same time.

Answer B is correct. Observing the entire process gives an employee knowledge of how functions impact other functions.

Answer C is wrong. High-quality customer service is about satisfying the internal and external customers.

Answer D is wrong. Systems management approach is a way to manage the different processes in the restaurant business.

Question 20

Answer A is correct. High-quality customer service will cause costs to decrease.

Answer B is wrong. Profits will be increased.

Answer C is wrong. Loyalty will be increased.

Answer D is wrong. Reputation will improve.

Question 21

Answer A is correct. Reconciliation is the process of matching recorded sales against actual payments received.

Answer B is wrong. Service-profit chain shows the relationship between revenue and growth.

Answer C is wrong. Service recovery is dealing with customer complaints.

Answer D is wrong. Fraud is an issue when dealing with credit or debit card payments.

Question 22

Answer A is wrong. Employees other than trainees receive products and services.

Answer B is wrong. Employees other than managers receive products and services.

Answer C is correct. Employees are customers to other people within the organization.

Answer D is wrong. The external customer is the end receiver of the service.

Question 23

Answer A is wrong. Customers may be loyal but don't always want the type of food or service provided by your restaurant.

Answer B is correct. Loyalty means the customer will choose your restaurant over other restaurants that provide the same type of food or service.

Answer C is wrong. Loyal customers may have a bad experience and may share it but still remain loyal if it was an exception or taken care of properly.

Answer D is wrong. Loyal customers may forgive one or two bad dining experiences but they will not remain loyal if bad service is continuous.

Question 24

Answer A is wrong. Suggestive selling does not replace reading the menu.

Answer B is wrong. A customer may be more likely to order dessert if they know it's available.

Answer C is correct. Suggestive selling is beneficial to the customer if it provides something they would not otherwise have had.

Answer D is wrong. Suggestive selling should not be the only chance a customer has to talk to the server.

Question 25
Answer A is wrong. The food cost ratio is 50%. (4/8=.5)
Answer B is correct. Food cost ratio is the percentage of sales that is spent on food supplies. It is calculated by dividing the cost by the revenue. (4/12=.33 or 33%)
Answer C is wrong. The food cost ratio is 25%. (4/16=.25)
Answer D is wrong. The food cost ratio is 20 %. (4/20=.20)

Question 26
Answer A is wrong. Credit card use does not change the normal tip policy.
Answer B is wrong. The manager does not need to be involved in the process.
Answer C is correct. The signature should be checked to help avoid credit card misuse.
Answer D is wrong. Return the card to the owner.

Question 27
Answer A is wrong. Comment cards are intended for external customers.
Answer B is wrong. Regular customers would probably only fill out a card if something changed or if they were dissatisfied. This would put them in the category of having a negative experience.
Answer C is correct. Customers who are upset are willing to take the time to let someone know.
Answer D is wrong. Satisfied customers usually do not bother to fill out a card unless something was above and beyond what they expected.

Question 28
Answer A is wrong. The policy may be for each employee to own the complaints and resolve them whenever possible.
Answer B is wrong. The person who has spent the most time with the customer is not necessarily the best person to handle the particular complaint.
Answer C is wrong. The purpose is to return the customer to a state of satisfaction. Blame is not an issue.
Answer D is correct. In order to be successful the employees need to understand who should handle complaints and how they should be handled.

Question 29
Answer A is wrong. An exchange occurs after a transaction has been completed and involves changing one item for another.
Answer B is wrong. A return is when an item is returned and money is given back to the customer.
Answer C is correct. A line item void occurs before payment has been received.
Answer D is wrong. Reconciliation matches recorded sales against actual payments received.

Question 30
Answer A is correct. Supportive processes are the elements that impact your internal customers to help them perform their jobs and be satisfied. The service-profit chain shows that when internal and external customers are satisfied costs are reduced and productivity is increased.
Answer B is wrong. Input-output relationship means one group receives product or service from another. These relationships have nothing to do with these programs.
Answer C is wrong. These programs do not support any financial programs. They are related to employee development and the workplace.
Answer D is wrong. OSHA requirements are safety regulations.

Customer Service Glossary

Cash overage   when you have more cash in the drawer than the POS system or register says you should have.

Cash shortage   when there is not enough cash in the registers once they have been reconciled with sales.

Cost ratio   the relationship of an operating cost to another financial figure.

Comment cards   a way to solicit immediate feedback from the guest about the dining experience.

Compensation   various programs and practices of employee reward and recognition, including benefits, incentive programs, flexible schedules, and rewards programs.

Competitive analysis   gathering information about the products, prices, and services of your competitors and drawing conclusions about how they affect your business.

Competitive point of difference   a perceived or actual difference between any two things that can be used to influence a customer's buying decision.

Consumer research   methods of investigation that are directed at discovering the products and services customers want and are willing to buy.

Cost-benefit ratio   the dollar value of benefits divided by the dollar value of the costs necessary to achieve those benefits.

Customer   anyone who is influenced by or has influence on a product, service, system, or process.[1]

Customer loyalty   customers prefer your restaurant to all similar restaurants.

Cycle of service   the accumulation of all the moments of truth for a guest from beginning to end of a dining visit.

Demographic analysis   customer data, such as age, education, socioeconomic group, location, family type, home type, income, etc. from consensus reports and special research to form customer subgroups.

External customer   the end receiver of a product or service and is outside the boundaries of an organization.

Field of experience   consists of all the things a person has gone through that affect either forming or interpreting a message.

Focus groups   face-to-face meetings of customers or potential customers who are asked to react to or comment on a topic of interest.

Forms of payment   cash, check, money order, credit or debit card, gift certificate, etc.

Four rights   a way to hire, train, compensate, and retain employees, which will enable you to satisfy them and achieve internal service quality.

High-quality customer service   consistently exceeding customers' expectations for products and the nature of services received, and for personal interaction during the delivery, to create value for the customer and profit for the organization.

Hospitality   *how* services are performed; the feeling that customers take with them.

---

[1]Juran, Joseph. A. Blanton Godfrey. *Juran's Quality Handbook,* 5th Edition, McGraw Hill, 1998.

Input-output relationship   any interaction between two people or two groups where the work product of one is used by the other.

Internal customer   anyone inside an organization who receives products, services, or information from someone else to complete his or her work.

Job design   the specific characteristics of a job.

Moment of truth   "any episode in which the customer comes into contact with any aspect of the organization and gets an impression of the quality of its service." [2]

Mystery shoppers (or secret shoppers)   consultants or employees who visit an operation, act as normal guests, and secretly report to management on the food, service, facility, and the experience.

Objective methods   gathering information without using a person whose interpretation or memory of what was said could change the feedback.

Process   a series of operations (tasks) that bring about a result.

Receiver   the person who gets the sender's message in the communication process.

Reconciliation   the process of matching recorded sales against actual payments received.

Secret shoppers (or mystery shoppers)   consultants or employees who visit an operation, act as normal guests, and secretly report to management on the food, service, facility, and the experience.

Sender   the person who has a message to communicate in the communication process.

---

[2]Albrecht, Karl. *At America's Service: How Corporations Can Revolutionize the Way They Treat Their Customers*. Homewood, IL; Dow Jones-Irwin, 1988.

Service   *what* restaurant and foodservice employees provide; it is a measure of the efficiency and effectiveness of their actions.

Service recovery   an operation's response to a complaint to return to a state of customer satisfaction.

Service-profit chain   how profit and revenue growth are linked in a high-quality customer service system.

Standard   describes criteria for items, tasks, behaviors, practices, and other aspects of an operation that represent the norm for your business.

Standard deviation   a data analysis method that measures how far a response is from the mean.

Statistical analysis systems (SAS)   systems used to tabulate and collate research data. SAS procedures use descriptive analysis methods to analyze data.

Suggestive selling   recommending additional or different items to a customer.

Survey   a series of specific questions an operation asks about one or more topics such as menu, food, service, decor, etc.

System   a set of standards, processes, and tasks that work together in an organized way to achieve an end result.

Systems management approach   a way to look at the activities in your operation as a group of different processes and tasks that work together to meet both the objectives of each process and of the whole operation.

Task   a responsibility, function, or procedure that is performed as part of a process.

Test marketing   try out actual products or services on real customers, often in a limited geographic area so as to minimize cost and risk.

Tools and equipment   essential resources needed for employees to effectively do the job.

Void   when a cash register entry has to be corrected by canceling the entry and entering the correct item.

Workplace design   the facility, the front of the house, and the back of the house.